بسم الله الرحمن الرحيم

The Woman, the Righteous Mother

Mothers in the Age of Modernity

Shaykh Dr. Ḥasan al-Balūshī

al-Burāq

سُورَةُ الفاتِحَةِ

بِسۡمِ ٱللَّهِ ٱلرَّحۡمَٰنِ ٱلرَّحِيمِ ١
ٱلۡحَمۡدُ لِلَّهِ رَبِّ ٱلۡعَٰلَمِينَ ٢
ٱلرَّحۡمَٰنِ ٱلرَّحِيمِ ٣ مَٰلِكِ يَوۡمِ ٱلدِّينِ ٤
إِيَّاكَ نَعۡبُدُ وَإِيَّاكَ نَسۡتَعِينُ ٥ ٱهۡدِنَا
ٱلصِّرَٰطَ ٱلۡمُسۡتَقِيمَ ٦ صِرَٰطَ ٱلَّذِينَ أَنۡعَمۡتَ
عَلَيۡهِمۡ غَيۡرِ ٱلۡمَغۡضُوبِ عَلَيۡهِمۡ
وَلَا ٱلضَّآلِّينَ ٧

Copyright

ISBN: 978-1-956276-71-8
Printed and published by al-Burāq Publications.
Translated and annotated by al-Burāq Publications.
Where needed, context and transliterations were added. Some minor edits were made to the translated Arabic text.

Ordering Information
We offer discounts and promotions for wholesale purchases, non-profit organizations, and other educational institutions. Contact us at the email below for further information.

al-Buraq.org
info@al-Buraq.org

First Edition | November 2025

Dedication

The publication of this book was made possible through the generous support of our donors.

Please recite *Sūrat al-Fātihah* and ask God for the Divine reward (*thawāb*) to be conferred upon the donors and also the souls of all the deceased in whose memory their loved ones have contributed graciously towards the publication of *The Woman, the Righteous Mother: Mothers in the Age of Modernity*.

We begin by giving all praise and thanks to God ﷻ for giving us the *tawfiq* to translate this book. He has guided us and without Him, we would not have been guided to the straight path embodied by the Prophet Muḥammad ﷺ and the Ahl al-Bayt عليهم السلام.

This book is dedicated to all the scholars, martyrs and believers who worked tirelessly to promote the pure Muḥammadan path. This book is also especially dedicated to Shaykh Ḥasan Jamāl Balūshī, who provided us with such a beneficial book. We pray God ﷻ grant him success in all of his noble endeavors.

We want to also give our thanks and appreciation to all believers from around the world and acknowledge the team which helped al-Burāq Publications complete this work, spending countless hours to make its publication possible. Please recite Sūrat al-Fātiḥah on behalf of them, their families, and their marḥūmīn.

This book is dedicated in honor of the following individuals. Please remember them in your prayers and may God ﷻ have mercy on them and their loved ones.

Duʿāʾ al-Ḥujjah

اللَّهُمَّ كُنْ لِوَلِيِّكَ الْحُجَّةِ ابْنِ الْحَسَنِ صَلَوَاتُكَ

عَلَيْهِ وَعَلَىٰ آبَائِهِ فِي هٰذِهِ السَّاعَةِ وَفِي كُلِّ

سَاعَةٍ وَلِيّاً وَحَافِظاً وَقَائِداً وَنَاصِراً وَدَلِيلاً

وَعَيْناً حَتَّىٰ تُسْكِنَهُ أَرْضَكَ طَوْعاً وَتُمَتِّعَهُ فِيهَا طَوِيلاً

O God, be, for Your representative, the Ḥujjat (proof), son of al-Ḥasan, Your blessings be upon him and his forefathers, in this hour and in every hour: a guardian, a protector, a leader, a helper, a proof, and an eye—until You make him live on the Earth, in obedience (to You), and cause him to live in it for a long time.

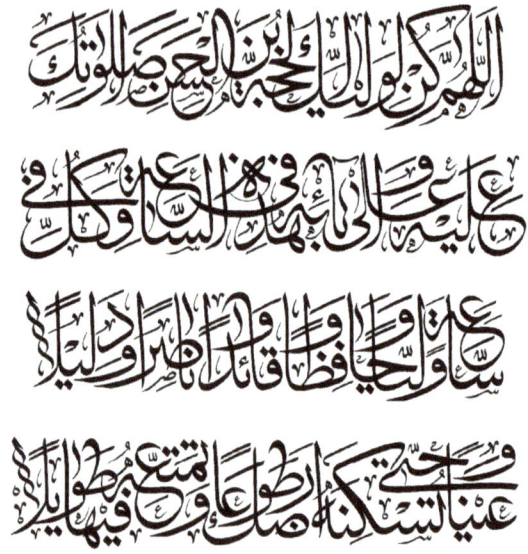

Terms of Respect

The following Arabic phrases have been used throughout this book in their respective places to show the reverence which the noble personalities deserve.

عزّ وجلّ

Used for God, meaning:
Exalted and Sublime (Perfect) is He

صلى الله عليه وآله وسلم

Used for Prophet Muḥammad, meaning:
Blessings from God be upon him and his family

عليه السلام

Used for a man (singular) of a high status, meaning:
Peace be upon him

عليها السلام

Used for a woman (singular) of a high status, meaning:
Peace be upon her

عليهما السلام

Used for men/women (dual) of a high status, meaning:
Peace be upon them both

عليهم السلام

Used for men and/or women (plural) of a high status, meaning:
Peace be upon them all

عجل الله تعالى فرجه الشريف

Used for Imām Muḥammad al-Mahdī, meaning:
May God hasten his return

قدس سره

Used for a deceased scholar, meaning:
May his resting [burial] place remain pure

Transliteration Table

The method of transliteration of Islamic terminology from the Arabic language has been carried out according to the standard transliteration table below.

ء	ʾ	ر	r	ف	f
ا	a	ز	z	ق	q
ب	b	س	s	ك	k
ت	t	ش	sh	ل	l
ث	th	ص	ṣ	م	m
ج	j	ض	ḍ	ن	n
ح	ḥ	ط	ṭ	و	w
خ	kh	ظ	ẓ	ه	h
د	d	ع	ʿ	ي	y
ذ	dh	غ	gh		
Long Vowels					
ا	ā	و	ū	ي	ī
Short Vowels					
ـَ	a	ـُ	u	ـِ	i

Table of Contents

Table of Contents 13

About the Author 1

Academic Qualifications: 1

Professional Experience: 1

Publications 2

Introduction 7

The Woman's Primary and Essential Identity 11

The Relativity of Identity 12

The Stability of Identity 13

The Identity of Woman 14

The Struggle over Women's Identity 40

The Righteous Mother: The Great Roles 47

Role One: Childbearing—The Secret of Life and the Creator's Craft 48

Role Two: Safeguarding the Generations' Health 51

Role Three: The Fount of Emotion and Its Warmth 58

Role Four: Managing the Home—An Elegant House and a Lively Atmosphere 61

How Do We Strengthen the Role of Motherhood in Our Society? 75

Pillar One: An Authentic Culture of Motherhood 76

Pillar Two: Educating and Preparing Mothers 79

Pillar Three: The Husband's Responsibility in Supporting Motherhood 81

Conclusion 87

About the Author

Academic Qualifications:

Shaykh Dr. Ḥasan al-Balūshī studied Islamic seminary sciences—from the introductory to the advanced levels—at the Ḥawzah of Imām al-Qāʾim عجّل الله تعالى فرجه الشريف between 2001 and 2009.

He obtained his PhD in Islamic Studies from the University of Exeter, United Kingdom, in 2015.

Professional Experience:

- Taught Logic, Uṣūl al-Fiqh (Principles of Jurisprudence), Arabic Language, and Fiqh (Jurisprudence) at the Ḥawzah of Imām al-Qāʾim between 2005 and 2009.

- Member of the Center for Studies and Research affiliated with the Ḥawzah of Imām al-Qāʾim.

- Member of the Organizing Committee of the Return to the Holy Qurʾān Conference held annually by the Ḥawzah of Imām al-Qāʾim, from its fifth session to the present.

- Member of the Editorial Board of al-Baṣāʾir, a quarterly journal for studies and research, since 2002.

- Has participated in numerous academic conferences and symposia.

Publications

Books in Arabic:

- *Philosophy of Ethics in Shīʿī Thought*
- *The History of Imāmī Uṣūl al-Fiqh*
- *The Ahl al-Bayt* ﻋﻠﻴﻬﻢ ﺍﻟﺴﻼﻡ *and Infallibility from Error: Theoretical Foundations and Practical Reality*
- *Steps Toward a Reading Society*
- *Imām al-Ḥusayn* ﻋﻠﻴﻪ ﺍﻟﺴﻼﻡ *in Our Spiritual Life*

Academic Papers in English:

- Beloushi, Ḥassan. "*The Paradigm Shift of Current Shīʿī Uṣūl al-Fiqh from the al-Bahbahānian Paradigm to Maqāṣid al-Sharīʿah.*" Presented at the Second Workshop of the Sharia Project: A UK–Netherlands Islamic Legal Studies Network, jointly convened by the University of Exeter and the University of Leiden, Exeter, April 2013.

- Beloushi, Ḥassan. "*The Philosophy of Education in al-Mudarrisī's Thought.*" Presented at The Ḥawzah Project, December 2011—a three-year collaborative project (2009–2011) between the British Society for Middle Eastern Studies (BRISMES) and the British Institute of Persian Studies (BIPS), sponsored by the British Academy, titled Clerical Authority in Shiʿite Islam: The Seminaries of Iraq and Iran.

- Beloushi, Ḥassan. "*Maqāṣid al-Sharīʿah Discourse in Contemporary Shīʿī Jurisprudence.*" Forthcoming as a chapter in an upcoming volume.

Research Papers in Arabic:

- *Attempts at Historicizing Imāmī Uṣūl al-Fiqh: A Preliminary Approach*

- *The Ethical Heritage in Shīʿī Thought: A Preliminary Approach*

- *The Ethical Heritage—A Methodological Approach: A Critical Reading of Foundational Premises and Research Methodologies*
- *The Establishment of Knowledge in the Islamic Context: Prospects for a Scholarly Way Out of the Impasses of Modernity*
- *The Bahbahānian Framework as an Interpretation of Modern and Contemporary Imāmī Uṣūl al-Fiqh: A Study of the Discipline's Development over the Past Three Centuries*

Translations:

- *Continuity and Creativity in Shīʿī Thought: The Relationship Between Akhbārism and the Tafkīk School*, by Prof. Robert Gleave.
- *Current Western Research on the History of Early Shīʿism*, by Prof. Robert Gleave.
- *The Science–Religion Debate: A General Introduction*, by John Polkinghorne.
- *Models of the Relationship Between Science and Religion*, by Denis Alexander.

- *The Anthropic Principle and the Science-Religion Debate*, by John Polkinghorne.

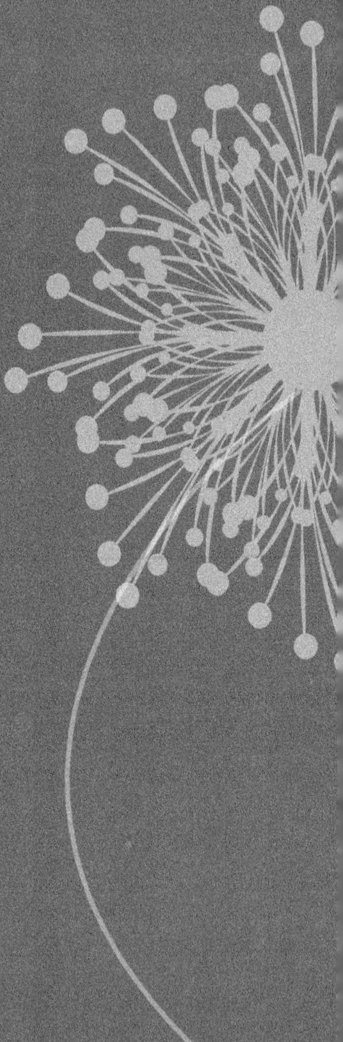

Introduction

بسم الله الرحمن الرحيم

In the Name of God, the Beneficent, the Merciful

Before you lies a discourse about woman as the blossom of the family, drawing many kinds of bees around her—she gives them to drink from her nectar so that they, in turn, may sweeten society with the honey they produce. It is a discourse about the mother—indeed, about the righteous mother.

In any case, it is not an easy discourse. On the one hand, it is a great subject—great because of the greatness of the one spoken about: the mother—the vessel of life, the bosom of affection, the heir to wholesome tradition, and much more besides. How can one encircle what is great?

On the other hand, it is a rugged discourse that swims against the rising current surrounding the notion of "woman"—a current that sees in her a business leader, svelte of figure, with few children, the man's coequal, bold of speech... and scant of modesty. How can a swimmer against the current be safe?

To ease these difficulties, I will begin with "the question of identity," asking: who determines the identities of things? Indeed, what is identity? How much of it is stable and how much changes? This then leads us to ask about the woman's first and essential identity. After that, I will turn to the mother's great roles—especially in forming the human person: as a child, as a youth, and then as a man—and to her role in managing the household, that noble yet taxing task that some women flee from in search of lighter exertion outside the home. I will conclude by speaking about everyone's responsibility to strengthen the role of motherhood in society—especially in the face of the opposing current—so that the true current may take its rightful course and place woman upon her glorious throne.

This discourse is, at root, an expansion and a measure of elaboration of a talk that God عز وجل granted me success to deliver from the pulpit of the Master of Martyrs عليه السلام in Muḥarram al-Ḥarām of the year 1446 AH. I judged—spurred and encouraged by some beloved friends—to edit it, deepen it, and elaborate certain parts of it, so that it might become a booklet that remains and endures longer than vocal letters do. May it be a treasure for me in the Hereafter, a benefit for our community, and a support and victory for the mother.

Written on the anniversary of the martyrdom of

Imam al-Ḥasan al-ʿAskarī ﷺ,

may my soul be his ransom,

Thursday,

8 Rabīʿ al-Awwal 1446 AH

12 September 2024 CE

Rumaythiyah, Kuwayt

The Woman's Primary and Essential Identity

The question posed here is: Is a human being's identity fixed or changeable? Who determines a human's identity? Indeed, what is identity?

Let us start with the last of these. In Arabic, when we answer the question "Who is he?" we are defining identity. It is a question that wants a determination of the nature of a thing, and from that nature, its function is determined. It is, then, a discussion of traits, properties, and distinguishing features that establish roles, functions, and responsibilities.

Likewise, in English, identity points to the self and its attributes; its Latin roots go back to "the selfsame thing."

But I regret to say that neither of these linguistic discussions yields much fruit, because the debate in reality is not linguistic but conceptual, intellectual, and cultural—and some might even fancy it philosophical. We face the question: how do we know a thing's properties and traits, and, consequently, its roles and responsibilities?

The Relativity of Identity

In response, some hold that things—and specifically the human being—do not have traits and roles that are discovered; rather, they are fabricated by the human being's own will—whether by his conscious, active will or his unconscious, passive will, which is affected by the deep and forceful pressures of society.

This approach makes identity optional—not merely at the level of cultural identity (which, within limits, is relatively open to choice), but even at the level of sexual identity, which defines the human being as male or female. Identity here is the outcome of a social construction—and at times a social power structure—that a person can transcend or resist to define his or her own identity.

Here, too, a thing's formative nature is not concomitant with its identity. Fruit—whose formative nature is nutritive—need not have feeding as its function; it could, instead, serve as a plaything in games and competitions.

Accordingly, the question about the essential identity of things is, on this view, a question devoid of meaning.

This has thrown the doors wide open in our age to transformations in people's identities and to movement from one identity to another, until matters have reached the point of male-female transitions in defining an individual human's identity, sexual inclinations, and social roles.

The Stability of Identity

By contrast, the second approach—and it is the sound one—holds that identity has an essential stability, while also allowing a margin for change that may be demanded by will, by social circumstances, or by cultural influence. The identity that determines the self, its roles, and its functions is not sheer personal choice nor a purely social-cultural formation.

Accordingly, the question of the essential identity of things—and particularly of the human being—is not only a legitimate question but a foundational one on which the destinies of social life and moral duties are built.

This stability, under the shade of religions and their teachings, granted humanity a flourishing stability for societies by stabilizing their basic building block, the family. And within its margin, it allowed relative change in social roles, but always turning on the axis of the constants.

With this clarification, we will have answered the three prior questions: identity is what determines the human self and its role and function; it is in a state of stability with a margin of change; and it is not hostage to the human being's pure will.

The Identity of Woman

Speaking of "the identity of woman" would not have been acceptable were it not for the storms of intellectual chaos that have blown over humanity in the past two centuries. A woman's identity had been clear, her roles delineated, her agency vibrant. But the allure of modernity—like any other allure—is intensely pleasurable in the moment and at the outset, then turbulent afterward and along the way, and in the end, a wound that does not heal.

Competing roles have been fabricated for women to the point that women have become bewildered about their identity, drawn now by one role and then by another. The question is posed anew, after strain and weariness, about her identity.

What we maintain here is that the woman's primary and essential identity is that she is a mother. After that—on the margin of the variables—other identities come, revolving first and foremost around motherhood.

We have four proofs for this: theological, biological, psychological, and social.

1. Theological Proof

By the theological (or doctrinal) proof, we mean this: God ﷻ has sovereignty, governance, authority, and will in determining human identity, its role, and its function. This is the meaning of servitude to the Creator, obedience to His prescriptive will, and absolute trust in His wisdom, knowledge, and excellent choosing.

Just as God ﷻ has irresistible sovereignty over how things are created and measured with their precise decree in the world of formation and nature—so that decrees run in the fairest form, the most beautiful crafting, and wondrous perfection—likewise in the world of human society and the social roles of the classes of people: He sketched them out with the hand of His wisdom so that people might live on earth by the scale of justice and beneficence, enjoy a goodly life here, and attain success in the Hereafter after fulfilling the moral role entrusted to them.

Trust in His wisdom and a deep sense of the human being's shortcoming drive a person to take refuge in the Lord ﷻ to aid him in ordering his affairs, determining his function, and valuing matters as they deserve—not to suppose that he knows better how to manage himself than his Lord ﷻ does.

Likewise, servitude to the Creator leads the human being to adhere to the limits of obedience and not to transgress the sanctum of the Lord ﷻ; nor to vie with God ﷻ in the sovereignty of His prescriptive Throne. This is the essence of divine authority (wilāyah), pure monotheism, and wearing the human being's majestic raiment of servitude.

Revelation is very explicit about women's identity as motherhood, in several ways:

First: Qur'ānic Indications

The Qur'ān abounds in indications of the maternal dimension in the female, as though to portray her basic, essential identity as a mother who performs the functions of motherhood. When the Noble Qur'ān mentions the female—whether with the term "mother" or "woman"—it predominantly, depending on the context, points first and foremost to the role of motherhood, its states, and its emotions. Even when the context is a mention of "woman," it points to what runs contrary to the role of motherhood or of being a wife, and in this, there is a strong intimation verging on explicit declaration of the female's essential identity, namely, motherhood. These indications include:

Indication One: The Mother of Mūsā—nursing, fearful, noble

When the Noble Qur'ān speaks of that noble female as the Mother of Mūsā ﷺ, it refers to her as a mother and highlights her maternal role.

It portrays the surging maternal emotions of a mother about to lose her infant while he is still in the cradle—she wants to complete his nursing, to fulfill her role, but it cannot be completed because of the looming danger from the killers. So the Lord reveals to her to cast him into the swelling river, promising that He will return him to her at the next nursing-time, removing thereby her fear and grief:

﴿وَأَوحَينا إِلىٰ أُمِّ موسىٰ أَن أَرضِعيهِ ۖ فَإِذا خِفتِ عَلَيهِ فَأَلقيهِ فِي اليَمِّ وَلا تَخافي وَلا تَحزَني ۖ إِنّا رادّوهُ إِلَيكِ وَجاعِلوهُ مِنَ المُرسَلينَ﴾

﴿wa-ʾawḥaynā ʾilā ʾummi mūsā ʾan ʾarḍiʿīhi fa-ʾidhā khifti ʿalayhi fa-ʾalqīhi fī l-yammi wa-lā takhāfī wa-lā taḥzanī ʾinnā rāddūhu ʾilayki wa-jāʿilūhu mina l-mursalīna﴾

﴿We revealed to Mūsā' mother, [saying], 'Nurse him; then, when you fear for him, cast him into the river, and do not fear or grieve, for We will restore him to you and make him one of the apostles'﴾[1]

She believed the revelation, placed him in the chest, and cast him into the river. Then other feelings surged within the mother—those of loss and emptiness—which the Qur'ān expressed as "emptying" (farāgh). From the pangs of these feelings, she was on the verge of divulging the great secret, but God fortified her heart. Such intensity would not have flared but for her deep instinct: that she was a mother:

[1] Sūrat al-Qaṣaṣ, Verse 7.

﴿وَأَصبَحَ فُؤادُ أُمِّ موسىٰ فارِغًا ۖ إِن كادَت لَتُبدي بِهِ لَولا أَن رَبَطنا عَلىٰ قَلبِها لِتَكونَ مِنَ المُؤمِنينَ﴾

﴿wa-ʾaṣbaḥa fuʾādu ʾummi mūsā fārighan ʾin kādat la-tubdī bihī law-lā ʾan rabaṭnā ʿalā qalbihā li-takūna mina l-muʾminīna﴾

﴿The heart of Mūsā' mother became desolate, and indeed she was about to divulge it had We not fortified her heart so that she might have faith [in God's promise]﴾[2]

But how can the mother's pain at losing her child be calmed except by meeting him, clasping him to her chest, and smothering him with kisses? Thus did God ﷻ do: He returned her child to her; the mother's moan quieted, and the child's tears were soothed:

﴿إِذ تَمشي أُختُكَ فَتَقولُ هَل أَدُلُّكُم عَلىٰ مَن يَكفُلُهُ ۖ فَرَجَعناكَ إِلىٰ أُمِّكَ كَي تَقَرَّ عَينُها وَلا تَحزَنَ﴾

---

[2] Sūrat al-Qaṣaṣ, Verse 10.

﴿idh tamshī ʾukhtuka fa-taqūlu hal ʾadullukum ʿalā man yakfuluhū fa-rajaʿnāka ʾilā ʾummika kay taqarra ʿaynuhā wa-lā taḥzana﴾

﴿When your sister walked up [to Pharaoh's palace] saying, "Shall I show you someone who will take care of him?" Then We restored you to your mother, that she might be comforted and not grieve﴾[3]

Indication Two: The female—and the yearning of motherhood

The Qur'ān tells us of a woman whose soul longed for motherhood and who awaited it for years upon years, until she despaired of herself. So when she was given good tidings of a child by the Great Creator, in Whose hand are the reins of all things, she could not contain herself but laughed—a wondrous expression of the mother's deep emotions. She is Sārah, the mother of the prophets of the Children of Israel:

﴿وَامرَأَتُهُ قائِمَةٌ فَضَحِكَت فَبَشَّرناها بِإِسحاقَ

وَمِن وَراءِ إِسحاقَ يَعقوبَ﴾

---

[3] Sūrat Ṭā Hā, Verse 40.

﴿*wa-mra'atuhū qā'imatun fa-ḍaḥikat fa-bashsharnāhā bi-'isḥāqa wa-min warā'i 'isḥāqa ya'qūb*[a]﴾

﴿*His wife, standing by, laughed as We gave her the good news of [the birth of] Isḥāq, and of Ya'qūb, after Isḥāq*﴾[4]

The Qur'ān even portrays her in another scene, striking her face in astonishment at what she was told:

﴿فَأَقْبَلَتِ امْرَأَتُهُ فِي صَرَّةٍ فَصَكَّتْ وَجْهَهَا وَقَالَتْ عَجُوزٌ عَقِيمٌ﴾

﴿*fa-'aqbalati mra'atuhū fī ṣarratin fa-ṣakkat wajhahā wa-qālat 'ajūzun 'aqīm*[un]﴾

﴿*Then his wife came forward crying [with joy]. She beat her face, and said, 'A barren old woman!'*﴾[5]

---

[4] Sūrat Hūd, Verse 71.

[5] Sūrat ad-Dhāriyāt, Verse 29.

Indication Three: The female—the vessel of the secret of life

The Qur'ān tells us of the mother's rank and her lofty station, to the point that she is the object of God's own injunction, alongside His injunction to monotheism. God ﷻ only issues an injunction when the matter is great and majestic. Why, then, the injunction regarding the mother? The Qur'ān explains that the female plays a tremendous role in pregnancy. In this, there is an indication of the identity of motherhood in the female by her undertaking this great task:

﴿وَوَصَّينَا الإنسانَ بِوالِدَيهِ حَمَلَتهُ أُمُّهُ وَهنًا عَلىٰ وَهنٍ وَفِصالُهُ في عامَينِ أَنِ اشكُر لي وَلِوالِدَيكَ إِلَيَّ المَصيرُ﴾

﴿wa-waṣṣaynā l-ʾinsāna bi-wālidayhi ḥamalathu ʾummuhū wahnan ʿalā wahnin wa-fiṣāluhū fī ʿāmayni ʾani shkur lī wa-li-wālidayka ʾilayya l-maṣīru﴾

﴿We have enjoined man concerning his parents: His mother carried him through weakness upon weakness, and his weaning takes two years. Give

thanks to Me and to your parents. To Me is the return﴾[6]

﴿وَوَصَّينَا الإِنسانَ بِوالِدَيهِ إِحسانًا ۖ حَمَلَتهُ أُمُّهُ كُرهًا وَوَضَعَتهُ
كُرهًا ۖ وَحَملُهُ وَفِصالُهُ ثَلاثونَ شَهرًا ۚ حَتّىٰ إِذا بَلَغَ أَشُدَّهُ وَبَلَغَ
أَربَعينَ سَنَةً قالَ رَبِّ أَوزِعني أَن أَشكُرَ نِعمَتَكَ الَّتي أَنعَمتَ
عَلَيَّ وَعَلىٰ والِدَيَّ وَأَن أَعمَلَ صالِحًا تَرضاهُ وَأَصلِح لي في ذُرِّيَّتي ۖ
إِنّي تُبتُ إِلَيكَ وَإِنّي مِنَ المُسلِمينَ﴾

﴾*wa-waṣṣaynā l-ʾinsāna bi-wālidayhi ʾiḥsānan ḥamalathu ʾummuhū kurhan wa-waḍaʿathu kurhan wa-ḥamluhū wa-fiṣāluhū thalāthūna shahran ḥattā ʾidhā balagha ʾashuddahū wa-balagha ʾarbaʿīna sanatan qāla rabbi ʾawziʿnī ʾan ʾashkura niʿmataka llatī ʾanʿamta ʿalayya wa-ʿalā wālidayya wa-ʾan ʾaʿmala ṣāliḥan tarḍāhu wa-ʾaṣliḥ lī fī dhurriyyatī ʾinnī tubtu ʾilayka wa-ʾinnī mina l-muslimīna*[a]﴿

﴾*We have enjoined man to be kind to his parents. His mother has carried him in travail, and bore him in travail, and his gestation and weaning take thirty months. When he comes of age and reaches forty*

[6] Sūrat Luqmān, Verse 14.

years, he says, 'My Lord! Inspire me to give thanks for Your blessing with which You have blessed me and my parents, and that I may do righteous deeds which may please You, and invest my descendants with righteousness. Indeed I have turned to you in penitence, and I am one of the muslims'[7]

Indication Four: The sanctum of the identity of motherhood in the female

To safeguard the identity of motherhood, to prevent tampering with it at the whim of human beings, and so that it not become a toy moved by people's cultures and moods, God عزّ وجلّ placed this identity within the sanctum of His sovereignty. He forbade any alteration of it by any human claim and deemed it fixed by the natural factors upon which He has run His ways. Thus, He forbade likening anyone to the mother in a way that would entail legal rulings upon him; He forbade ẓihār—a man's claiming that his wife is like his mother so that he will not approach her. Mother is a fixed reality by the biological cause of giving birth, not by some asserted cause arising from any quarter whatsoever:

[7] Sūrat al-Aḥqāf, Verse 15.

﴿الَّذينَ يُظاهِرونَ مِنكُم مِن نِسائِهِم ما هُنَّ أُمَّهاتِهِم ۖ إِن أُمَّهاتُهُم إِلَّا اللّائي وَلَدنَهُم ۚ وَإِنَّهُم لَيَقولونَ مُنكَرًا مِنَ القَولِ وَزورًا ۚ وَإِنَّ اللَّهَ لَعَفُوٌّ غَفورٌ﴾

﴿[a]lladhīna yuẓāhirūna minkum min nisā'ihim mā hunna 'ummahātihim 'in 'ummahātuhum 'illā llā'ī waladnahum wa-'innahum la-yaqūlūna munkaran mina l-qawli wa-zūran wa-'inna llāha la-'afuwwun ghafūr[un]﴾

﴿As for those of you who repudiate their wives by ẓihār, they are not their mothers; their mothers are only those who bore them, and indeed they utter an outrageous utterance and a lie. Indeed God is Excusing, Forgiving﴾*[8]

﴿وَما جَعَلَ أَزواجَكُمُ اللّائي تُظاهِرونَ مِنهُنَّ أُمَّهاتِكُم ۚ وَما جَعَلَ أَدعِياءَكُم أَبناءَكُم ۚ ذٰلِكُم قَولُكُم بِأَفواهِكُم ۖ وَاللَّهُ يَقولُ الحَقَّ وَهُوَ يَهدِي السَّبيلَ﴾

---

[8] Sūrat al-Mujādilah, Verse 2.

* A kind of repudiation of the marital relationship among pre-Islamic Arabs which took place on a husband's saying to his wife 'Be as my mother's back' (*ẓahr*; hence the derivative *ẓihār*).

﴾wa-mā ja'ala 'azwājakumu llā'ī tuẓāhirūna minhunna 'ummahātikum wa-mā ja'ala 'ad'iyā'akum 'abnā'akum dhālikum qawlukum bi-'afwāhikum wa-llāhu yaqūlu l-ḥaqqa wa-huwa yahdī s-sabīl[a]﴿

﴾nor has He made your wives whom you repudiate by ẓihār your mothers, nor has he made your adopted sons your sons. These are mere utterances of your mouths. But God speaks the truth and He guides to the way﴿*[9]

Indication Five: The female—the bosom of dignity

Time and again, the Noble Qur'ān points to the identity of motherhood in the female. Here, it indicates that the role of nurturing, care, tender rearing, and dignified treatment flows from the female because of her innate motherhood, even if she is not the biological mother. By virtue of this

---

[9] Sūrat al-Aḥzāb, Verse 4.

* A kind of repudiation of the marital relationship among pre-Islamic Arabs which took place on a husband's saying to his wife 'Be as my mother's back' (*ẓahr*; hence the derivative *ẓihār*). Concerning the revocation of such a divorce and the atonement prescribed, see 58:1–4.

deep instinct hidden within her, it manifests as soon as the occasion presents itself.

Thus, the Qur'ān tells us of that great woman who cared for God's prophet Mūsā ﷺ in Pharaoh's palace—how her heart inclined to the infant and the feelings of motherhood surged in her as soon as her eyes fell upon the little child the river had cast into her lap:

﴿وَقَالَتِ امرَأَتُ فِرعَونَ قُرَّتُ عَينٍ لِي وَلَكَ ۖ لَا تَقتُلُوهُ عَسَىٰ أَن يَنفَعَنَا أَو نَتَّخِذَهُ وَلَدًا وَهُم لَا يَشعُرُونَ﴾

wa-qālati mraʾatu firʿawna qurratu ʿaynin lī wa-laka lā taqtulūhu ʿasā ʾan yanfaʿanā ʾaw nattakhidhahū waladan ﴿wa-hum lā yashʿurūna﴾

﴿Pharaoh's wife said [to Pharaoh], '[This infant will be] a [source of] comfort to me and to you. Do not kill him. Maybe he will benefit us, or we will adopt him as a son.' And they were not aware﴾[10]

A similar scene is repeated with another woman who longed for motherhood, and the Lord

[10] Sūrat al-Qaṣaṣ, Verse 9.

delivered to her a youthful prophet; she honored him, and he became the leader of a state:

﴿وَقَالَ الَّذِي اشْتَرَاهُ مِن مِصْرَ لِامْرَأَتِهِ أَكْرِمِي مَثْوَاهُ عَسَىٰ أَن يَنفَعَنَا أَوْ نَتَّخِذَهُ وَلَدًا ۚ وَكَذَٰلِكَ مَكَّنَّا لِيُوسُفَ فِي الْأَرْضِ وَلِنُعَلِّمَهُ مِن تَأْوِيلِ الْأَحَادِيثِ ۚ وَاللَّهُ غَالِبٌ عَلَىٰ أَمْرِهِ وَلَٰكِنَّ أَكْثَرَ النَّاسِ لَا يَعْلَمُونَ﴾

﴿wa-qāla lladhī shtarāhu min miṣra li-mra'atihī 'akrimī mathwāhu 'asā 'an yanfa'anā 'aw nattakhidhahū waladan wa-ka-dhālika makkannā li-yūsufa fī l-'arḍi wa-li-nu'allimahū min ta'wīli l-'aḥādīthi wa-llāhu ghālibun 'alā 'amrihī wa-lākinna 'akthara n-nāsi lā ya'lamūn[a]﴾

﴿The man from Egypt who had bought him said to his wife, 'Give him an honourable place [in the household]. Maybe he will be useful to us, or we may adopt him as a son.' Thus We established Joseph in the land and that We might teach him the interpretation of dreams. God has [full] command of His affairs, but most people do not know﴾*[11]

---

[11] Sūrat Yūsuf, Verse 21.

* Or 'Keep him in a respectable manner.'

The Combined Indicators

Taken together, these indications point to—and at times explicitly declare—the woman's basic and essential dimension: motherhood. The Noble Qur'ān treats it as the presumed, fixed, enduring, and latent identity in woman, revealing the divine, law-like ordainment of human nature on its female side.

Second: The Moral Role

Here, the prescriptive will of God ﷻ becomes manifest, directing us toward the moral roles we are meant to undertake so that we realize the purpose for which we were created, succeed thereby in our test, and attain the good pleasure of the Lord ﷻ.

When we return to that prescriptive will—expressed through juristic directives in their categories of obligation, recommendation, dislike, and prohibition—we find that with respect to the female, it turns first and essentially to the roles of motherhood, being a wife, and building the family, whose axis is the righteous mother.

The Prophet's ﷺ Wives: Mothers of the Households

One model that ought to be an exemplar for Muslims is the Household of Prophethood, in its marital dimension. Thus God ﷻ directs this household to what it should be—specifically here, His direction to the woman in this household—asking of her modesty; circumscribed relations when speaking with others; and adherence to the responsibilities of the home—all within the framework of obedience to God ﷻ.

﴿يا نِساءَ النَّبِيِّ لَستُنَّ كَأَحَدٍ مِنَ النِّساءِ ۚ إِنِ اتَّقَيتُنَّ فَلا تَخضَعنَ بِالقَولِ فَيَطمَعَ الَّذي في قَلبِهِ مَرَضٌ وَقُلنَ قَولًا مَعروفًا﴾

﴾yā-nisāʾa n-nabiyyi lastunna ka-ʾaḥadin mina n-nisāʾi ʾini ttaqaytunna fa-lā takhḍaʿna bi-l-qawli fa-yaṭmaʿa lladhī fī qalbihī maraḍun wa-qulna qawlan maʿrūfan﴿

﴿وَقَرنَ في بُيوتِكُنَّ وَلا تَبَرَّجنَ تَبَرُّجَ الجاهِلِيَّةِ الأولىٰ ۖ وَأَقِمنَ الصَّلاةَ وَآتينَ الزَّكاةَ وَأَطِعنَ اللَّهَ وَرَسولَهُ﴾

﴾wa-qarna fī buyūtikunna wa-lā tabarrajna tabarruja l-jāhiliyyati l-ʾūlā wa-ʾaqimna ṣ-ṣalāta wa-ʾātīna z-zakāta wa-ʾaṭiʿna llāha wa-rasūlahū﴿

﴾O wives of the Prophet! You are not like any other women: if you are wary [of God], then do not be complaisant in your speech, lest he in whose heart is a sickness should aspire, and speak honourable words. Stay in your houses and do not display your finery with the display of the former [days of] ignorance. Maintain the prayer and pay the zakāt and obey God and His Apostle﴿[12]

The Nursing Mother

Among the legal rulings that the Noble Qurʾān details is a woman's nursing of her children, and in this, there is sufficient indication of a woman's essential maternal role. Nursing is an act that only woman performs. Part of nursing is obligatory upon her, and part recommended; and it is upon the man to provide the sustenance required for the mother to carry out this role.

---

[12] Sūrat al-Aḥzāb, Verses 32–33.

﴿وَالوالِداتُ يُرضِعنَ أَولادَهُنَّ حَولَينِ كامِلَينِ ۖ لِمَن أَرادَ أَن يُتِمَّ الرَّضاعَةَ

﴿wa-l-wālidātu yurḍiʿna ʾawlādahunna ḥawlayni kāmilayni li-man ʾarāda ʾan yutimma r-raḍāʿata﴾

﴿Mothers shall suckle their children for two full years, —that for such as desire to complete the suckling﴾[13]

Here, the father's role comes in to provide sustenance:

﴿وَعَلَى المَولودِ لَهُ رِزقُهُنَّ وَكِسوَتُهُنَّ بِالمَعروفِ ۚ لا تُكَلَّفُ نَفسٌ إِلّا وُسعَها ۚ لا تُضارَّ والِدَةٌ بِوَلَدِها وَلا مَولودٌ لَهُ بِوَلَدِهِ ۚ وَعَلَى الوارِثِ مِثلُ ذٰلِكَ ۗ فَإِن أَرادا فِصالًا عَن تَراضٍ مِنهُما وَتَشاوُرٍ فَلا جُناحَ عَلَيهِما ۗ وَإِن أَرَدتُم أَن تَستَرضِعوا أَولادَكُم فَلا جُناحَ عَلَيكُم إِذا سَلَّمتُم ما آتَيتُم بِالمَعروفِ ۗ وَاتَّقُوا اللَّهَ وَاعلَموا أَنَّ اللَّهَ بِما تَعمَلونَ بَصيرٌ﴾

﴿wa-ʿalā l-mawlūdi lahū rizquhunna wa-kiswatuhunna bi-l-maʿrūfi lā tukallafu nafsun ʾillā

---

[13] Sūrat al-Baqarah, Verse 233.

*wusʿahā lā tuḍārra wālidatun bi-waladihā wa-lā mawlūdun lahū bi-waladihī wa-ʿalā l-wārithi mithlu dhālika fa-ʾin ʾarādā fiṣālan ʿan tarāḍin minhumā wa-tashāwurin fa-lā junāḥa ʿalayhimā wa-ʾin ʾaradtum ʾan tastarḍiʿū ʾawlādakum fa-lā junāḥa ʿalaykum ʾidhā sallamtum mā ʾātaytum bi-l-maʿrūfi wa-ttaqū llāha wa-ʿlamū ʾanna llāha bi-mā taʿmalūna baṣīr*un﴿

﴾*and on the father shall be their maintenance and clothing, in accordance with honourable norms. No soul is to be tasked except according to its capacity: neither the mother shall be made to suffer harm on her child's account, nor the father on account of his child, and on the [father's] heir devolve [duties and rights] similar to that. And if the couple desire to wean, with mutual consent and consultation, there will be no sin upon them. And if you want to have your children wet-nursed, there will be no sin upon you so long as you pay what you give in accordance with honourable norms, and be wary of God, and know that God sees best what you do*﴿[14]

---

[14] Sūrat al-Baqarah, Verse 233.

The Woman as Mother… and the Man as Provider

Among the legal rulings God ﷻ has imposed upon the family is that the man be the father who spends on his dependents—including his wife—so that she does not need to secure her living in a way that would force her to work and leave the home, leading to a falling short in the dimension of motherhood.

Thus, the mother becomes a source of repose for the family:

﴿وَمِن آياتِهِ أَن خَلَقَ لَكُم مِن أَنفُسِكُم أَزواجًا لِتَسكُنوا إِلَيها وَجَعَلَ بَينَكُم مَوَدَّةً وَرَحمَةً ۚ إِنَّ في ذٰلِكَ لَآياتٍ لِقَومٍ يَتَفَكَّرونَ﴾

﴿wa-min ʾāyātihī ʾan khalaqa lakum min ʾanfusikum ʾazwājan li-taskunū ʾilayhā wa-jaʿala baynakum mawaddatan wa-raḥmatan ʾinna fī dhālika la-ʾāyātin li-qawmin yatafakkarūn[a]*﴾*

﴾And of His signs is that He created for you mates from your own selves that you may take comfort in them, and He ordained affection and mercy between

you. There are indeed signs in that for a people who reflect﴾[15]

Many other legal rulings uncover the woman's essential, divinely ordained role—embodied in motherhood.

2. The Biological Proof

Does a thing's form indicate its function? Or is the relationship severed between the forms and constitutions of things and their functions? What if the form did not come about randomly but by the prior will of a Wise One—can we, then, infer a function from what the Wise Maker did in His crafting?

We have many examples of this in our daily lives. When a new machine appears—made by a company renowned for its skill and intelligence in designing machines to perform specific functions—would it be reasonable to separate the machine's components and outward form from the function for which it was made?

---

[15] Sūrat ar-Rūm, Verse 21.

So it is in the world of human creation: the biological differentiation between the sexes is exceedingly clear—within each sex as well, across the stages of life. One does not need a precise specialization in biology and physiology to grasp the evident reality of this differentiation.

All one needs is native intelligence and a rational commonsense to infer that a woman is biologically created as a "mother": she is the fetus's vessel and its first home for formation and growth. Thereafter, she is the primary source of its nourishment through nursing. Everything in her body—externally and internally—exists primarily to perform the functions of motherhood.

That is when we speak in general understanding and rational fitrah. But if we sail into the specialized sciences and precise knowledge, we will encounter wonders in the precision of wise formation, every part of which points to the fact that this being is a mother.

3. The Psychological Proof

It is that deep yearning—that innate instinct in the female soul—to be a mother. She is created upon an instinctive comportment that proceeds from her not by accident or happenstance, but because of an essential reality within her: caring for and attending to the child; long patience with him; nurturing him; saturating him with affection; anxiety over him; protecting him with all the strength she has; sacrificing for his sake; encouraging him in times of trial—all of this is not incidental in the female's behavior; rather, these are essential acts.

When she is deprived of motherhood, the female feels a vast and deep emptiness, which she seeks to compensate for by undertaking maternal roles with other children, or social responsibilities of the same kind, such as teaching in nurseries, volunteering to serve orphans, and the like.

This is not a cultural behavior produced by the passage of days and their habits, or by civilizations and their practices, nor one fashioned by males through their dominance, as certain feminist trends like to portray it. Rather, it is an essential constitution in the female soul which the All-Powerful, All-Wise Creator placed within her, to paint the tableau of a life made whole among its members.

4. The Social Proof

The female is distinguished by social behaviors in which she differs from the male. Their clarity has led some social writers to depict the matter as though women came from the planet Venus and men from Mars.

Such social behaviors cannot be mere temporary accidents or purposeless play without wisdom; rather, they are part of the grand tableau of wondrous creation.

When we reflect on them, we find they converge upon behaviors of empathy and care. A woman is a being who expresses her emotions conspicuously—whether joy through modes of celebration, sadness through tears that do not soon run dry for her, sympathy through touch and embrace, or constriction through grumbling and complaint.

She is also a being who attends greatly to details—in remembering them, noticing them before her, speaking about them, and taking care of them. The literature of social psychology overflows in this field. I will point to one study as a sample from this scientific domain teeming with findings.

It is a study on women's acuity in noticing others' outward appearance compared with that of men. A study was conducted in 2004 by several researchers and published in the journal Personality and Social Psychology Bulletin, volume 30, issue 2, of the Society for Personality and Social Psychology in Washington, United States of America—one of the most important research organizations in this field. The study was entitled: "Gender Differences in Memory for the Appearance of Others." It sought to answer the question: Do gender differences affect acuity in noticing details? The question arose from a long-standing debate among psychologists and cognitive scientists about the effect of gender differences on this mental function. In this study[16], five extensive experiments were conducted to verify the matter. The result was that women are more accurate than men in noticing details in others' appearances—reflecting one aspect of women's concern for more information.

She is also a being who displays her emotional bonds clearly and expresses them in diverse ways, so

---

[16] Horgan, T. G., Mast, M. S., Hall, J. A., & Carter, J. D. (2004). *Gender Differences in Memory for the Appearance of Others*. Personality and Social Psychology Bulletin, 30(2), 185196-.

that her emotion is intense and manifest and is communicated to others in a saturating manner.

These social behaviors—some of which we have mentioned—ultimately pour into empathy and care, which qualify her for the great role of motherhood, the tending of the family, and the creation of a wonderful atmosphere in the home.

The Struggle over Women's Identity

In 2022, through social media platforms—and while people were weary from the consequences of the frightening pandemic, COVID-19—the world woke to a shocking, surprising documentary entitled What Is a Woman?, presented by the American platform The Daily Wire and hosted by the conservative political activist and media figure Matt Walsh.

The answer to this question may seem self-evident to the vast majority of people, but the profound shock was that scientific and intellectual elites found themselves unable to answer this question, to the point of bewilderment.

The documentary included interviews with several experts in psychology, medicine, and politics, as well as interviews with members of the general public. Walsh poses a simple question—"What is a woman?"—and seeks to explore the diverse answers the participants offer. The film places considerable focus on the ongoing debate over gender identity and gender transition, and it raises questions about the impact of these concepts on society, especially in relation to upbringing and education. Through the film, Matt Walsh seeks to show that there are large disparities in how people understand sex and gender identity—and the focal point of this debate is "woman."

This film is but a simple reflection—like the tip of an iceberg in the ocean—of a profound struggle over the human being's moral identity, and specifically over women's identity. For a long time now, multiple fields have been in confusion, bewilderment, and even manifest error in studying women and determining their identity.

It is also a reflection of a civilizational struggle between divergent values concerning the human being, including women. This struggle is translated into massive media and cultural instruments. In their ultimate sum, they aim to redefine the human being—and, in particular, woman—in a way that makes her everything except motherhood and "mother."

Whoever does not notice this struggle—its chapters, tools, soldiery, platforms, and standards—and does not hear its drums of war is heedless and deeply asleep, as though in a world other than our own.

The female is distinguished by social behaviors that differ from those of the male—a difference so evident that some social writers have portrayed the matter as though woman came from the planet Venus, while man came from Mars.

Motherhood
The Essential Identity of Woman

The Arguments upon which this concept is Based

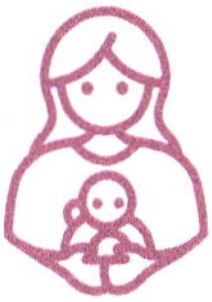

1 The Theological (Religious) Argument

Motherhood is regarded as a central pillar of feminine identity, as reflected in numerous Qur'ānic verses.

2 The Social Argument

The female is distinguished by social behaviors that differ from those of the male and correspond to the role of motherhood—such as empathy, attentiveness to detail, and emotional connectedness.

3 The Biological Argument

The woman's physical and functional constitution is designed in a way that corresponds to her role as a mother.

4 The Psychological Argument

A woman experiences a deep yearning to become a mother, accompanied by an instinctive inclination toward nurturing and caring for the child.

Childbearing is an expression of divine creativity in the process of creation—a process belonging exclusively to God, exalted is He, in which none of His creation shares. God ﷻ has made the womb of woman the vessel that carries this magnificent divine secret, thereby honoring her with this noble mission.

The Righteous Mother: The Great Roles

It is an age-old problem in human thought: how can we appraise intangible matters, great roles, and lofty virtues? If you quantify them in numbers, you underpay their due; if you praise them with all the arts of encomium, you do not reach their true commendation.

Who can appraise the martyr's blood, the laborer's sweat, the scholar's inkwell, or the friend's stand in the time of distress? How then can we appraise what is greater than all that—the mother's role?

Some attempt to portray the greatness of the mother's role (or "work," as they like to call it) by comparing it to the most strenuous forms of labor, to bring the picture closer.

Backbreaking work—however intense—is limited to working hours; but a mother's work is twenty-four hours a day, seven days a week (24/7). Whereas strenuous work is confined to a set time, it also has a defined schedule; but the mother's work has no schedule—nighttime vigils and daytime toil. Whereas strenuous work is bounded by certain psychological pressures that relate to the nature of the job, the mother faces pressures without defined bounds and from diverse sources. If strenuous work requires dealing with particular parties, the mother must deal with many: children, adolescents, and adults; males and females; the husband and his family; her parents and their connections—and she must manage all these relationships successfully. While the strenuous worker expects a material return, the mother gives without limit and without return. Finally, the technical, managerial, and intellectual skills required in the most demanding jobs are limited, but the mother is required to possess diverse social, emotional, technical, organizational, and nutritional skills, broad information, and continual learning.

I will enumerate here some of the great roles the righteous mother undertakes.

Role One: Childbearing—The Secret of Life and the Creator's Craft

The first of the great roles borne by the righteous mother is childbearing. Contrary to other cultures —especially contemporary ones—that consider pregnancy and childbirth to be a heavy burden upon the woman, seeking to reduce them as much as possible and to minimize their pains, the divine,

God-centered perspective in Islam looks upon childbearing from multiple angles:

First: The Secret of Life

Childbearing is an expression of divine creativity in the process of "creation"—a process that belongs to God ﷻ alone, in which He associates none of His creation. God ﷻ made the woman's womb the vessel that embraces this tremendous divine secret, honoring her with this noble task. By carrying this sacred secret, the woman attains a great station within the holy order of creation.

God's honoring the woman by granting her the capacity to bear children is not a mere biological role; it is a symbol of the human worthiness that shoulders this divine dignity. In the woman's womb, the first formation of life begins—the first heartbeat that represents one of the greatest secrets of the cosmos. This places the woman at the forefront of the procession of creation: she is the vessel in which the earliest stages of human existence are cradled.

This process carries a profound symbolism indicating that woman is not merely an instrument for childbearing; rather, she is the object of a special divine solicitude: He placed within her the capacity to tend and form life. Childbearing, at its core, ties the woman directly to the sacred act of creation, granting her a unique measure of worthiness and responsibility in life.

In the end, this divine honoring signals the greatness of the role woman plays in the continuity of humankind—a sacred role suffused with the meanings of love, care, and sacrifice—an extension of God's creativity manifest in the very process of creation.

Second: Striving in the Path of God ﷻ

God ﷻ has set pregnancy and childbirth on a par with striving (jihād) in His path. Just as jihād is a praiseworthy hardship, with immense reward, a great opening, and a wide victory for society, so too are pregnancy and childbirth. Though they involve hardship, their reward is great; they are an adornment for society and a reinforcement for it with young men and women who are the heartbeat of its life.

In a ḥadīth from the Messenger of God ﷺ:

> O Umm Salamah, when a woman becomes pregnant, she has a reward like one who strives with his person and wealth in the path of God. When she gives birth, it is said to her: 'Your sin has been forgiven—resume your deeds.' When she suckles, then for every suckling she has the freeing of a slave from among the descendants of Ismāʿīl.[17]

Role Two: Safeguarding the Generations' Health

The second of the righteous mother's great roles is her bearing responsibility for the community's public health. This role is one of those hidden tasks that affect society deeply and over the long term, yet cannot be precisely measured and may even be neglected by some.

The truth, however, is that a society's health and safety begin with the mother, and that is in three stages:

Stage One: Before Birth and During Pregnancy

---

[17] Ṭūsī, Shaykh Muḥammad b. Ḥasan, *al-Amālī*, p. 618.

It has become axiomatic today to speak about the mother's role in the child's health while she is carrying him. What the mother eats passes directly to her fetus; the more mindful the mother is of her health and of good nutrition, and the more she is in a state of psychological stability and physical fitness before and during pregnancy, the more that affects her newborn.

Thus, we find that the Prophet ﷺ who is the Seal of the Prophets, came with the best of religions and was occupied with teaching people many matters; among the things the Prophet ﷺ spoke to the community about was: what should a woman eat during her pregnancy? For example:

> The Messenger of God ﷺ said:
>
> > God never sent a prophet nor a legatee except that from him was found the scent of quince; so eat it and feed it to your pregnant women—your children will turn out well.[18]

[18] Majlisī, ʿAllāmah Muḥammad Bāqir, *Biḥār al-Anwār*, Vol. 62, p. 177.

Reports in this field are numerous. This is merely by way of example and reminder—to call people to consider what they provide their wives during pregnancy, and to alert mothers to seek more knowledge about what benefits their fetuses in this critical period of the child's life.

Stage Two: After Birth

In Islamic jurisprudence, nursing is given a wide scope of attention. It is not confined to being a mere biological feeding process; rather, it extends to constitute a great role in the child's life and in shaping his psychological and social being. Nursing is an inherent right of the child; in some cases, it may even be regarded as a duty upon the mother-in-law, indeed a right of the husband over her as well. Here, I do not wish to speak in the language of religious obligations, but rather about the mother's role in offering comprehensive care through nursing her child, a role that goes beyond nourishment to encompass psychological and emotional dimensions.

In jurisprudence and in science alike, nursing is defined as not merely a biological interaction between mother and child; it is a multi-dimensional act that touches the depths of the human constitution. Alongside its clear health effects, nursing is also a gateway to forging deep emotional bonds between mother and child—bonds that enrich the child's inner life and nourish his spirit. This complex interaction between mother and child develops the child's social aspects, endows him with confidence, and plants within him a sense of security—paving the way for the formation of his future personality.

Some psychologists tend—somewhat exaggeratedly—to hold that the first three years of the child's life are decisive in building his personality, with a large portion of his lifelong traits being set therein. Perhaps this is what the Prophet Muḥammad ﷺ affirmed when he said:

> When a mother nurses her newborn, she has the reward of one who strives with his person and wealth. When she gives birth, her sin is forgiven; and when she nurses, then for every suckling she has the freeing of a slave from among the descendants of Ismāʿīl.[19]

This noble Prophetic ḥadīth points to the great value of nursing—not only from the bodily

[19] Ṭūsī, Shaykh Muḥammad b. Ḥasan, *al-Amālī*, p. 618.

standpoint, but also in terms of the spiritual and moral reward the parents attain.

If nursing continues for two full years, as religious teachings recommend, it goes beyond its biological role to become an emotional and spiritual journey between mother and child. It is not mere feeding; it is a fabric of tenderness and reassurance woven through every suckling, whereby the mother conveys to her child love and care. This process is not only nourishment for the body but nourishment for the spirit, which grants it unparalleled importance in building the child's personality.

Hence, the emphasis on caring about nursing and about wet nurses. The Commander of the Faithful عليه السلام said:

> Look to whom you entrust the nursing of your children, for the child grows up according to it.[20]

[20] Rayshahrī, Āyatullāh Muḥammad, *Mīzān al-Ḥikmah*, Vol. 20, p. 1088.

And he also said:

> Choose for nursing as you choose for marriage, for nursing changes dispositions.[21]

Stage Three: Early Childhood

Early childhood is the cornerstone upon which the child's future health is built. During this stage, bodily and mental growth are at their peak, and they depend to a great extent on the care the child receives. The mother plays a principal role in this growth: she monitors her child's health and is keen to provide appropriate nutrition and necessary medical care. Through regular doctor visits and required vaccinations, the mother ensures the child's protection from disease and supports him to grow up in a healthy environment. Her role is not confined to providing food; it extends to psychological and emotional care as well—something that strengthens the child's holistic development and lays a firm foundation for his future.

The dietary habits the child learns in his early years form the basis of his future health, and the mother

---

[21] Ibid.

is responsible for shaping these habits. By providing healthy and varied meals, the mother introduces the child to different kinds of food. She instills in him eating patterns that will remain with him throughout his life, to the point that some find nothing in existence more delicious than their mother's cooking. The mother's choice of healthy food bolsters his physical and mental growth, whereas offering unhealthy foods may negatively affect his health and development.

The mother's dietary choices for the child directly influence his physical and mental health. Providing balanced meals rich in nutrients helps support brain function and sound physical growth. Conversely, excessive consumption of fast food can lead to long-term health problems such as obesity and weakened immunity. Thus, the mother's decision to choose healthy food becomes a fateful decision that determines how robust and healthy the child will be in the long run.

Through this great role, the mother becomes the primary source of public health for society and for generations to come.

Role Three: The Fount of Emotion and Its Warmth

From the moment the infant emerges from his mother's womb and is placed upon her chest—while she is exhausted to the point of collapse from the strains of labor and delivery—the first language of emotion between the mother and her newborn begins. The child addresses her with his eyes and his cry, asking for her compassion and tenderness; the mother answers him with her embrace, her kisses, and her touch, responding to him.

The matter is more complex than that. A human being's personality is formed of multiple dimensions on the psychological plane, and at a very early period, going back to those first moments of his cry and weeping, and to the mother's pattern of dealing with him in those early times. Psychologically, a human being needs to feel safety and compassion, as well as to sense esteem and respect. These components are deep within the human soul, grave in their shaping, and they extend with him for many years. Thereafter, he may feel stable regarding them, or many people may be heedless of their lack of such components, resulting in unhealthy behaviors. Few are those who are granted the success to perceive the deficiencies within themselves and who strive to compensate for them or to repair their personalities.

Here, the mother has a very great role, and at a very early stage, in forming these components in a precise balance that culminates in a personality that is sound, emotionally and psychologically stable.

The matter is more complex still: the issue is not confined merely to shaping these psychological and emotional components, but extends to what is called "emotional regulation"—that is, sound, proper handling not only of the self, but of its own reactions with itself (such as anxiety, tension, anger, and feelings of frustration) and its responses with others (such as feelings of jealousy, of being overpowered by others, surges of emotion, and even generosity of soul in dealing with peers and forming friendships).

In all these matters, and others besides, the mother plays a great and critical role—if she attends to it and fulfills it as required.

By contrast, a child's sense of neglect; not receiving the necessary attention; being left for long periods without care; failure to respond to his emotions or emotional needs; constant anger against him and shouting in his face; resorting to behaviors of emotional deprivation; or delegating his care to others without follow-up or direct attention—all of these pour into negative directions that directly affect the child.

This mode of dealing leaves deep imprints upon the child's psyche. It leads to the deterioration of his relationship with himself and with others, and weakens his trust in his surroundings and in himself. Continuous neglect and failure to respond to his emotional needs generate in him a sense of isolation and rejection—planting the seeds of psychological disorders such as anxiety or depression in later stages of his life.

Moreover, subjecting the child to repeated anger or shouting creates an environment filled with tension and psychological pressure, which affects his ability to express his emotions healthily. Deprivation—whether emotional or material—contributes to forming a sense of deficiency or inferiority in him, something that may be reflected in his social and academic behavior.

These negative methods leave long-term effects: they not only impact the child's emotional development, but they also touch his ability to adapt to future life challenges—making him more prone to problems of self-confidence, social communication, and even academic success.

Role Four: Managing the Home—An Elegant House and a Lively Atmosphere

A home, for a human being, is not like any shelter for the rest of creatures: it is not merely a place to ward off heat or cold, or to sleep and eat. It is a stage upon which the human soul interacts with others in elevated human relations—where fatherhood and motherhood, sonship and siblinghood, and the marital bond meet in a wondrous weave. Here, food becomes a symbol of everyone's efforts: a father's compassion toward the family; a mother's tenderness in preparing and cooking it; and a wholesome connection among the household members who take part in weaving this daily tale.

The sitting room is not merely a place for passing gatherings; it is a cradle of intimacy and affection where conversations and memories meet and where debates and discussions are sparked. It is a stage for deep human connection. As for the bedrooms, they are not merely havens for dreams: for the spouses, they are a chamber of love and affection, carrying within them the secrets of partnership and intimacy; and for siblings, their rooms represent a human partnership that brings them together in wholesome empathy and an unbreakable fraternal bond. In these corners, the home pulses with life, and human giving appears in its most splendid forms.

We would not be exaggerating to say that the righteous mother is the axis of this home and the one chiefly responsible for its atmosphere, its order, and its table. She is the center of giving and organization, and the essential pillar in building the family. A report transmits that Fāṭimah عليها السلام sat before the Messenger of God ﷺ to seek his judgment—not because of a dispute between her and ʿAlī عليه السلام, but to define duties and limits. She asked him about the bounds of her role and those of ʿAlī عليه السلام. The Messenger of God ﷺ ruled for them that everything outside the house was the task of ʿAlī b. Abī Ṭālib عليه السلام, and everything inside the house was the task of Fāṭimah عليها السلام.

From Abū ʿAbdillāh, from his father عليهما السلام:

> ʿAlī and Fāṭimah brought their case to the Messenger of God ﷺ concerning service. He

judged for Fāṭimah that her service was within the door, and judged against ʿAlī what was beyond it. Fāṭimah said:

> None knows what joy entered me except God, when the Messenger of God ﷺ spared me the burden of men's necks.[22]

And Abū Jaʿfar al-Bāqir said:

> Fāṭimah guaranteed for ʿAlī the housework—kneading, baking, and sweeping the house—and ʿAlī guaranteed for her what was beyond the door: carrying firewood and bringing food.[23]

Let us detail these dimensions.

First: The Home Atmosphere

A home's atmosphere is hostage to the mother's acumen in creating and shaping it. She can turn the walls of a house into a kingdom of love and tranquility, where feelings are embodied in every

---

[22] Burūjirdī, Āyatullāh Sayyid Ḥusayn, *Jāmiʿ Aḥādīth al-Shīʿah*, Vol. 20, p. 234.

[23] Ibid.

corner. With her intelligence and prudence, she creates a comfortable, warm environment, making the house a refuge for both father and children. She understands each person's needs and can adapt to them with tact and feeling, making each one sense that this place is where he can find repose and serenity.

It is related from al-Zahrā' ﷺ that she said to 'Alī ﷺ:

> The house is your house and the free woman is your wife; do as you wish.[24]

The mother is the one who draws the father back home after a long day of work. Rather than the house being merely a place to sleep and eat, she turns it into a place he longs for—where he finds comfort and kindness, and can shed the pressures of daily life. She greets him with a pure smile and a kind word, melting away the day's fatigue and filling him with positive energy.

---

[24] Majlisī, 'Allāmah Muḥammad Bāqir, *Biḥār al-Anwār*, Vol. 28, p. 303.

This accords with what is related from ʿAlī ﷺ:

> I would look at her, and my worries and sorrows would vanish at my gaze upon her.[25]

Likewise, children find in the mother their source of happiness and their reason to return home. She provides them with safety and love; she organizes their time and encourages their personal and emotional growth. In her embrace, they feel attention and care, and she turns the home into an environment that fosters emotional and social development.

The mother does not content herself with daily caretaking; she is distinguished by her ability to create an atmosphere of geniality and affection. She knows how to kindle sparks of laughter, lighten tensions, and build bridges of amity among family members. With her creativity, she establishes household activities that strengthen family bonds —whether recreational or educational—so that the house becomes more than a dwelling: it is the nucleus of deep human relationships.

---

[25] Ibid., Vol. 42, p. 134.

Second: Cleanliness and an Elegant Home

The home is a canvas reflecting the mistress of the house's taste; its cleanliness and order are the mother's elegant brush with which she paints, through her refinement and taste, the details of the family's life. Cleanliness is not merely a daily duty; it is a silent giving, like a breeze that fills the corners with comfort and calm. The elegant mother is artful in ordering every corner of her home: floors gleam, fabrics breathe in softness, and small details —such as flowers arranged in the corners—add a touch of renewed life. She knows that a single touch of tidiness or cleanliness is enough to transform an ordinary house into a comfortable kingdom.

Nor does it stop there: these calm, orderly surroundings have a significant impact on children's behavior and ease of mind. A child who grows up in a home where order and cleanliness are the rule learns, indirectly, to value them in his own life and among his friends. For example, when children return from school to find their rooms tidy and their beds clean, with fragrant sheets, they feel cared for and at ease—something that strengthens their sense of psychological stability.

By these acts—however simple they may seem—the mother amasses great reward. In Islam, every effort expended for the family, from cleaning to organizing, is a devotion for which one is rewarded. When a mother cleans the kitchen after preparing a warm meal or rearranges the toys after a long day of play, she is performing a noble role for which God recompenses her. From Abū ʿAbdillāh ﷷ:

> Umm Salamah asked the Messenger of God ﷺ about the merit of women in serving their husbands. He ﷺ said:
>
> > No woman lifts anything in her husband's house from one place to another, intending thereby good order, except that God looks upon her, and whomever God looks upon, He does not punish.[26]

Because of her fine-grained nature, a woman is the family's first interior designer. She knows where to place the cushions to add a warm touch to the sofa; she chooses curtain colors that catch the morning sun; she arranges books on the shelves like a work of art. She makes the house an unforgettable place,

---

[26] Ṭūsī, Shaykh Muḥammad b. Ḥasan, *al-Amālī*, p. 618.

where all find themselves in the warmth of her gentle touch.

Thus, the house becomes more than a shelter: rooms are no longer merely places to sleep or eat but spaces pulsing with warmth and care. In every corner, her touches reflect a deep love for her family members. The house is then no longer silent walls; it is fresh air carrying the scent of attentiveness and tenderness.

In contrast to modern houses that have become structures devoid of spirit, the human home becomes a space full of life, where all feel a sense of belonging and comfort. With her artistic touches, the mother fashions a place where father and children find tranquility and where memories are created that nourish the soul and endure forever.

Third: A Goodly Table . . and a Human Gathering

At the table around which we gather daily, food is not merely a meal to stave off hunger; it is a place for hearts to meet, for stories to be told, for worries to be aired—and at times a high-level family conference to discuss thorny issues. There, eyes speak through their glances; smiles embrace through laughter; and sometimes tears share in their flowing sympathy.

From the Prophet ﷺ:

> The most beloved food to God is that upon which the hands of many believers multiply.[27]

The undisputed lady of the table is the righteous mother—she who knows how to satisfy the variety of her children's tastes: this one is picky, that one prefers citrus, another eats healthfully, and the father's moods are changeable. In each dish, she considers a particular desire, combining various flavors with skill, pleasing everyone, and filling the table with warmth and love.

It is related from al-Ṣādiq ؑ that he said:

> No woman gives her husband a drink of water except that it is better for her than a year's worship.[28]

---

[27] Majlisī, ʿAllāmah Muḥammad Bāqir, *Biḥār al-Anwār*, Vol. 59, p. 290.

[28] al-Ḥurr al-ʿĀmilī, Shaykh Muḥammad, *Wasāʾil al-Shīʿah*, Vol. 20, p. 172.

She is the lady of the table because she sets the traditions of dignity, the etiquette of dining, and the rules of cleanliness: all food is treated nobly; there is no wastefulness in eating; and each person is responsible for the cleanliness of his place.

She is also the lady of the table because she creates an atmosphere of intimacy, maintains the table's calm, and lends it a touch of liveliness and warmth. By her presence, the table becomes a space of comfort and harmony—where the children's laughter and the elders' discussion are in tune—so that intimacy prevails and the peace is realized, making every moment around the table an unforgettable memory.

By contrast, in these days—owing to the absence of the righteous mother—the table seems to have lost its original luster, becoming merely a silent piece of furniture in a corner of the home. Food once served as a bridge that brought hearts together; now it has become a routine devoid of spirit. Each person sits alone, face lit by the dull glow of screens. The father is absorbed in his work, phone in hand, fingers moving without pause, as though the meal before him were merely a side task in a crammed day. The mother watches the scene in heavy silence, wondering how the moments that used to gather them turned into this desolate stillness.

In the kitchen, the maid prepares food without spirit—a repetitive process day after day. Dishes are served as if they were material objects devoid of the family's warmth. The children eat while immersed in their virtual worlds—no conversation, no exchange of glances. The screens speak in their stead, severing those hidden bonds that once gathered them around the table.

Food has become for satiety only, not for gathering. Instead of the table being a stage for love and intimacy, it has become a stage for silence and isolation—each one eating in his own seclusion, as though they were strangers under one roof.

The Great Roles of Woman

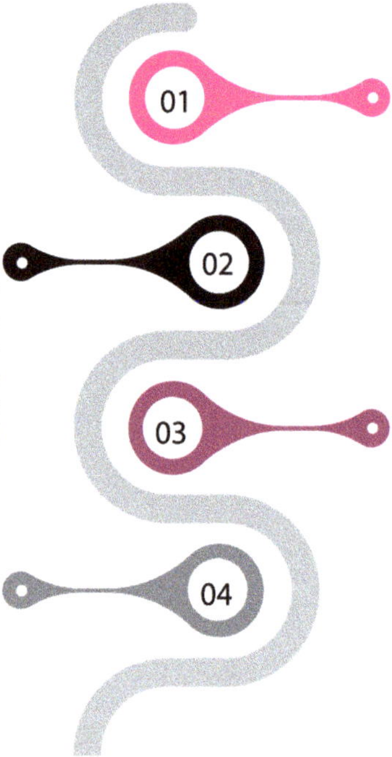

The First Role: Childbeari
The Secret of Life and
Creator's Artistry

Childbearing represents the m
exalted of woman's roles, for G
ﷻ honors her by making her
vessel of life — the beare
creation and divine creati
Pregnancy and childbirth
thus regarded as stations of ji

The Second Role
Ensuring the Physical Well-being of Generations

The mother cares for her child's health before birth, during nursing, and throughout his growth, providing him with sound nourishment infused with affection and psychological care.

The Third Role
The Source and Warmth
Affection

The mother is the first sou
of emotion and love. S
shapes the child's emotio
personality and nurtu
within him a sense of secur
and self-worth.

The Fourth Role
Managing the Home
Creating Elegance and Vital Atmosphere

The mother cultivates a home environment of tranquility and comfort, strengthening the family bonds among its members and fostering harmony within the household.

In contrast to modern houses that have turned into lifeless structures, the human home becomes a space brimming with vitality — a place where everyone feels a sense of belonging and comfort. Through her artistic touch, the mother creates an environment where the father and children find tranquility, and where memories are born that nourish the soul and remain alive forever.

How Do We Strengthen the Role of Motherhood in Our Society?

What has been mentioned is no more than a glimpse of the great role the righteous mother plays in her home and with her children, and of the deep effects that extend to society as a whole. Though we have tried to highlight the greatness of this role, I admitted at the outset of this booklet that words may fail to capture the essence of the mother's role.

What must be noted is that this essential role of motherhood needs support and enhancement—especially in the face of secondary roles promoted by contemporary, materially oriented cultures. The need for support arises from the fact that the roots of motherhood in our society remain firmly and deeply planted by innate disposition—and more deeply so in the environment of Islam, where values reinforce this fitrah. Support thus strengthens those wholesome roots and stands by them in the face of challenges.

The need for enhancement stems from the need to keep pace with changes without compromising the essence of motherhood. Enhancement means a new formulation of the mother's role in modern molds suited to social and intellectual changes, without losing the original spirit of this role.

Accordingly, we can point to three fundamental pillars for supporting and enhancing motherhood in our societies:

Pillar One: An Authentic Culture of Motherhood

Although motherhood is a firmly rooted instinct in a woman's conscience, like any innate instinct, it is liable to distortion and alteration, and at times may even be inverted from what it once was. This transformation occurs primarily through intellectual and cultural influence, whereby a woman's convictions change gradually: entrenched principles are eroded, fundamentals are altered, and values recede—then behavioral change comes as a secondary reaction. With the passage of time, fitrah may be effaced or grossly deformed.

In our contemporary world, the pace of cultural influences upon individuals has accelerated: ideas and orientations pour into minds from every direction. Minds have become a constant target of divergent intellectual currents, employing methods that combine shock with gradual acclimation.

These influences invade both the visual and intellectual senses at once, such that the human being finds himself facing a great, invisible battle, often stripped of his intellectual weapons and defenses.

This battle is not merely a confrontation with ideas or concepts; it is a battle targeting the distortion of human fitrah in general—and motherhood in particular—since motherhood is among the most important pillars on which society's structure rests. Preserving and protecting the fitrah of motherhood requires continuous intellectual and cultural support, so that this fitrah remains pure and able to grow and flourish in an environment that reinforces its values and shields it from every kind of tampering.

From this vantage point, cultural and intellectual backing for motherhood is a fundamental pillar for strengthening its role and grounding its worth in society. This support is a practical application of the dictum "establishing the right"—for sound and noble ideas always need ongoing reinforcement. They are not merely self-standing truths that settle by themselves; they need those who will buttress, amplify, and reiterate them so that they remain present in the collective consciousness and can resist attempts at alteration or distortion.

In this context, society must adopt innovative, multifaceted means of supporting these ideas—means that do not stop at limited, traditional channels, but extend to all cultural and media platforms. For example, mass media can be used to spread awareness and strengthen a positive image of motherhood through television programs, public-service announcements, and moving stories. Likewise, the cinematic arts play a major role in shaping public opinion: films and series can present strong, inspiring models of motherhood aligned with sound societal values.

In addition, public competitions and community dialogues can be activated as tools to elevate the value of motherhood and underscore its pivotal role in building society. Such activities encourage direct engagement with the public and help create open conversations about the importance of motherhood in society and its role as a foundational pillar in raising the coming generations.

Accordingly, cultural and intellectual support for motherhood becomes an integrated process encompassing media, the arts, community competitions, and other instruments that help keep this idea alive and renewed amid contemporary challenges.

Pillar Two: Educating and Preparing Mothers

The arena of competition among diverse cultures today is no longer at the middle or advanced stages of people's lives; it has descended to early childhood—into what is planted there of concepts, ideas, and visions—through "soft" tools such as children's games and films, and "hard" tools such as ongoing formal education and its content.

The mother we want—righteous and able to undertake her great roles—does not take shape in the house of marriage; rather, she ferments and is formed in the early years of childhood. The role expected of her is planted in her intellectual and emotional conscience through modes of upbringing that seek to ready her to be a mother before anything else.

The family is the first station where the basic values and principles of motherhood are formed, as the girl learns through observation and imitation. The mother presents a living model of care and tending, offering indirect lessons in love, devotion, and sacrifice. In this setting, the role of motherhood is naturally rooted within the girl until it becomes an inseparable part of her personality and of her emotional and intellectual formation. The family's discourse to her—that she is soon to be a mother—also plays its part in shaping motherhood early on. So too do the household roles assigned to her—maintaining the home's cleanliness, the arts of cooking, and caring for younger siblings: all of this is framed as "training courses" for the great role to come.

These seeds broaden to find their space in educational programs that play a pivotal role in forming a girl's awareness of her identity and future responsibilities. Through school activities and pedagogical curricula, the girl is reinforced in the concepts of care, cooperation, empathy, and household management. Educational stories and group projects give her the chance to explore the mother's role from a leadership angle, where she grasps the mother's importance in raising generations and building communities. Here, the school is not merely a place for learning, but a space for shaping character and preparing for the role of motherhood with love and awareness.

Community programs complete this preparation by organizing workshops and interactive activities that encourage girls to absorb the role of motherhood in practical ways. Social clubs, associations, girls' centers, mosques, and ḥusayniyyahs provide platforms for discussion and learning where experiences are exchanged across generations and true stories are presented that underscore the importance of this role. In this way, motherhood is redefined as a collective responsibility to which the family, the school, and the community all contribute—so that the girl is presented to her future role with a deep vision and an awareness of the importance of her impact in building a stable, flourishing future.

Pillar Three: The Husband's Responsibility in Supporting Motherhood

The tree of motherhood cannot grow, flourish, and bear fruit without the support and care of fatherhood, represented in the family by the husband. The family is a human partnership between a man and a woman, and neither can thrive without the other. It is like a taut rope held at either end by a man and a woman—the rope will surely fall if either lets go.

This is the meaning of "pairedness" in all things: it is built upon a complementary duality in which each supports the other. In family life, this duality grows stronger and more bonded.

That is in normal circumstances. In our time—given the sharp challenges facing the family—this duality, mutual support, and ongoing cooperation are even more urgent. Material enticements encircle the husband like a bracelet girds a wrist, and worldly lures of frivolous living swirl around the woman like a raging cyclone that steals away her heart. Under such conditions, a mother's task will be near impossible if she is left alone in the arena to fulfill her motherhood as it ought to be.

Here, precisely, the husband-father's role emerges: his material support through reasonable maintenance that allows the woman to be a mother dedicated to her motherhood and her great role; and his moral support through patience and forbearance—and through full conviction that the being to whom he is joined—the woman—was created to be a mother before anything else. All that is in her which the husband might have thought was "for him," in accordance with God's law and pure fitrah—namely, the lawful mutual enjoyments between the spouses—is in truth a passing guest entrusted to her; in reality, she was created to tend the child to come in her womb. Without such conviction, the husband-father may become the primary discourager of his wife's becoming a mother, for she will remain torn between staying that enchanting young woman for him—sacrificing her motherhood for that—or moving to her true role, with its natural consequences of sacrificing contemporary "beauty" standards displayed by the media.

Pregnancy and childbirth have bodily and psychological consequences; nursing means nights of vigil and days of toil; caring for children at times entails exhaustion. All this will seem "at the husband-father's expense"—yet in truth it will be to his account, not from his account, if conviction in the righteous family and in complementary roles is in place.

This never means the matter is between two extremes—either "be a mother" or "be the princess of your husband." Rather, the intelligent woman

—helped by her husband—can be the princess of her home, her husband, and her children.

Strengthening and Supporting the Role of Motherhood in Society

The Authentic Culture of Motherhood

- Protecting the innate human nature (fiṭrah).
- Intellectually and culturally supporting noble ideas.
- Activating media initiatives and awareness programs.

Educating and Preparing Mothers

- The Importance of Family and Early Education
- Preparing young girls for the role of motherhood.
- Community activities and educational workshops.

The Husband's Responsibility in Supporting Motherhood

- The husband is a fundamental partner in the success of motherhood.
- He provides both material and emotional support.
- Cooperation is essential in facing family challenges.

The tree of motherhood cannot grow, flourish, and bear fruit without the support and care of fatherhood—represented by the husband within the family. This is because the family is a human partnership between man and woman; neither of them can truly thrive without the other.

Conclusion

At the outset of this booklet, I said I was swimming against the current. Here I am, concluding this swim—hoping I have made it to the shore of safety, and hoping even more that I have managed to accompany with me others who were swimming with the current, or at least made them notice that there is a safe and comfortable shore—one with repose and happiness—and convinced them that swimming against the current is possible, and in many cases is the right course.

The Commander of the Faithful, ʿAlī b. Abī Ṭālib عليه السلام, says:

> Do not feel desolate on the path of truth because of the fewness of those who tread it.[29]

And the noble Imam Mūsā b. Jaʿfar al-Kāẓim عليه السلام says:

> O Hishām! If there were a walnut in your hand and people said it is a pearl, that would not benefit you when you know it is a walnut; and if there were a pearl in your hand and people

---

[29] Majlisī, ʿAllāmah Muḥammad Bāqir, *Biḥār al-Anwār*, Vol. 67, p. 107.

said it is a walnut, that would not harm you when you know it is a pearl.[30]

[30] Ibid., Vol. 20, p. 126.

www.ingramcontent.com/pod-product-compliance
Lightning Source LLC
Chambersburg PA
CBHW051325120626
46547CB00015B/2393
9781956276718